AF006589

Samara Bedwell's

11 keys to success as a landlord

Investor quick read

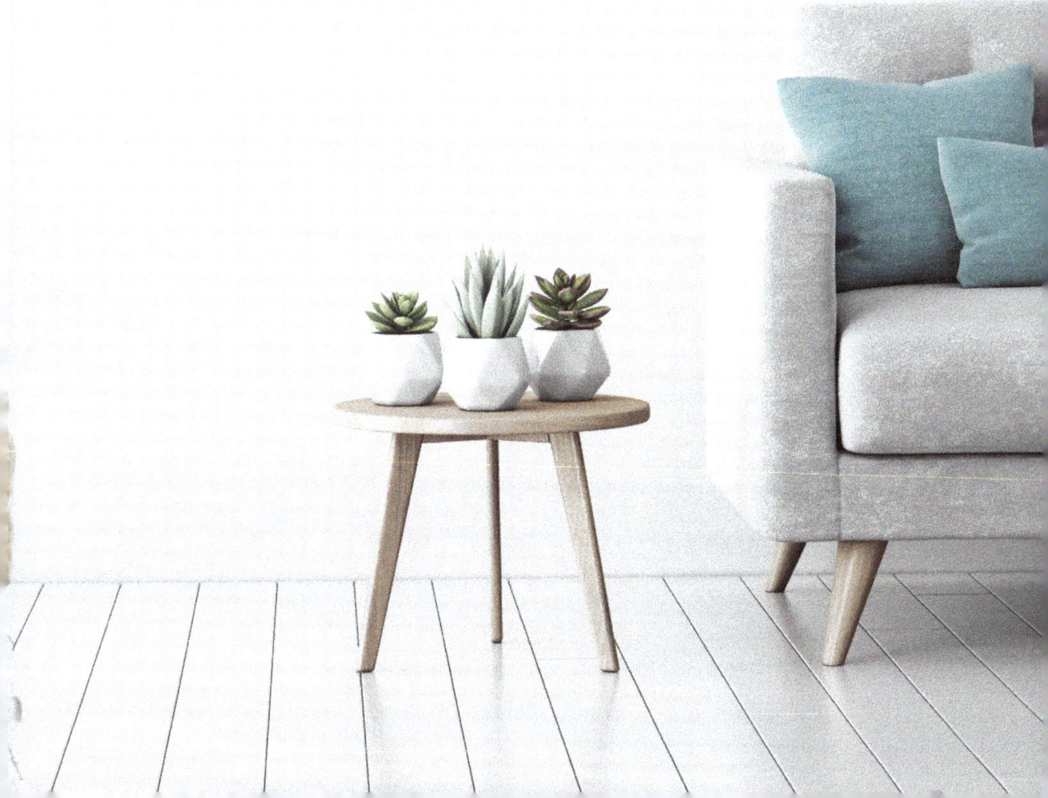

Thank you for acquiring a copy of this book. I hope you will find the information helpful during your property investment adventure.

About Samara Bedwell

Samara is the Managing Director of Macwell Property Management and has 17 years' experience in the industry. During her career she has won many national and state industry awards.

In 2001, Samara left her home in the country to train and work in Brisbane as a property management assistant for Raine & Horne. Young and ambitious, she flourished in the "big smoke" and within 12 months she was the senior property manager of the department – generating massive growth and consistently winning industry awards.

In 2010, Samara moved on to establish and manage the property management department for a major builder/developer from the ground up, gaining valuable people management skills and strong business acumen.

Highly regarded as an industry expert in Queensland, Samara has written several key articles for industry publications and newspapers. She is known for exceeding expectations in customer service and believes in employing staff with a positive, hard-working attitude.

When I was a property manager, a lot of clients came to me with little-to-no understanding of what to do after purchasing their investment property. While their decision to purchase was right, they were unaware of their rights and responsibilities as property owners, and were unsure of how to get the investment working for them. When it came to taking that next step, some drew a blank, others were uninformed, and a few were still reeling from the actions of agents who were involved in the sale. Not surprisingly, the investments were not working as they should have.

> *Everything seems complicated and confusing*

I heard many clients say: "Everything seems complicated and confusing." Well, here's the good news: it's not. This book, in its easy-to-read format, shows you just how straightforward it is.

Generally, we purchase an investment property for financial gain and future stability. Before you can rest on your laurels, however, you need to ask the question: "How do we make this property work for us and what do we need to do as investors to get the returns we want from our purchase?"

When researching for this book, I found a lot of literature explaining how and where to buy investment properties. I also found there was very little information out there to help us know what we do once we have bought an investment property.

This book will address the key points of property investment: keeping your investment property, getting the desired return, and being aware of the implications and requirements of being a landlord.

Life would be easy if you could purchase an investment property and sit back and reap the rewards. Unfortunately, it's not quite that simple – but it doesn't have to be hard either.

Like any investment there is a certain level of risk associated with buying a property. We are going to discuss the highs and lows, the benefits, some legislation requirements, and ways to sustain your investment property regardless of what market conditions look like.

This book is designed to be an easy-to-understand guide first-, second-, or third-time investors can grasp. Not everyone will agree with all of my ideas, but all I ask is that you read this book with an overall open mind and take away and act on those areas you find interesting.

What I am not going to discuss is where the hot spots to buy are, and what you need to do to finance yourself into the market. I am simply focussing on the process that takes place once you have bought your investment property, and how to make it work for you.

Let's get started:

Contents

Key 1	Every person has their trade: Apointing a property manager	07
Key 2	Establishing a depreciation schedule and understanding the other tax benefits of owning an investment: What no one tells you about	17
Key 3	Insuring your property: What options are there?	21
Key 4	Pricing your property and marketing your home	33
Key 5	Presentation: You don't get a second chance to make a first impression	37
Key 6	Securing a tenant: Get the best pick of the bunch	43
Key 7	Maintaining that tenant: A little respect goes a long way	47
Key 8	Property maintenance: During the tenancy, sometimes you have to spend a little to make a lot	51
Key 9	Property maintenance: Between tenancies, you can make mutton look like lamb	55
Key 10	How can you make money from your property?	59
Key 11	The round up	63

Key 1

Every person has their trade: Appointing a property manager

The most successful investors I know have adopted a business mindset in regards to their investment property portfolios.

However, I have been witness to some people who purchase a property and treat it like a hobby. In my experience, these people don't tend to achieve maximum return and benefits from their investment.

To be a successful property investor, you need to create plans and strategies on how you are going to proceed – a little like a business plan. Surround yourself with industry experts and other successful landlords and engage professionals to provide research and market information. These people will point you in the right direction.

Enlisting a successful property management team is one of the most important and beneficial decisions you can make to ensure your portfolio grows and your assets appreciate. An experienced property manager will help you maximise the benefits of your property regardless of the rental market.

For the most part, it is commonly thought a property manager simply collects the rent, prepares lease agreements, secures tenants, and assists in repairs and maintenance. While these are important aspects of a property manager's role, the behind-the-scenes truth is they do – or at least should do – a lot more. A good property management team will be up-to-date with the various Acts regarding tenancies in their state, as well as legislation that impacts property, landowners and tenants. In each state, rules and regulations are named differently, but common legal requirements incorporate fire and safety acts, residential tenancies acts, codes of conduct, pool acts, fencing laws, and anti-discrimination acts, along with legal professions, trust accounting, and consumer protection.

An experienced property manager will help you maximise the benefits of your property regardless of the rental market.

One of the biggest responsibilities a property manager has is to mitigate all loss on behalf of the landlord client. Property management has now become a very specialised industry and has a huge focus on risk management.

Finding an agent that fits with your unique needs can seem a daunting task, especially for new investors. After all, there are many competing agencies to choose from and, unfortunately, until you try one it can be hard to see how they fit with your needs. It's a great idea to start by talking to other investors who may be able to recommend an agent that has helped them achieve success. However, if you find yourself on your own, here are a couple of tips on what to do and how to get started:

- Research the internet to find agencies that service your area. This does not necessarily mean it has to be an agent based in your suburb, as current technologies now allow property management businesses to cover larger areas.
- Look for agents who are recognised by the industry and have won awards within their company or from state-based real estate institutes, for example, the Real Estate Institute of Queensland (REIQ).
- A professional property management division will have a clear, user-friendly web page that is up-to-date and informative. Avoid tardy or out-dated pages as this is generally a good indication of how progressive the agency is and how much attention they are likely to put in to marketing their business and your investment property. Marketing will become one of the most important attributes an agency can offer when the time comes for finding tenants for your investment property.

After you have narrowed down your search to a few or several agents, prepare a list of functions that are important to you that your property management team should possess. Use this list as a questionnaire or a checklist.

Conduct phone interviews of these agencies. Often, the department manager or property manager won't be available to receive your call, but don't discount the office – request a return call by leaving your details and explaining what the call is regarding. If after 48 hours your call has not been returned by the agency, consider disregarding the agent and move on to the next. A sense of urgency is an absolute must in property management. All enquires must be responded to promptly. Failure to do so could mean the team is unreliable, staff are incompetent, or the division is unable to service the needs of their clients due to workload – this would not be a good agency to get involved with.

Here a few questions you might like to ask the department manager or property manager:

How long have they been a property manager?

How many properties do they manage?

Do they engage external professional consultants to help take the department to the next level?

What formal training have they undertaken?

What procedural systems do they have in place? (If possible, request to see a copy of any standard forms or checklists used within the office to minimise human error.)

Do they attend regular training courses to keep up-to-date with legislation and industry changes?

Are they a member of the Real Estate Institute?

How do they communicate with property owners? (Do they publish regular newsletters or send letters when there has been a change in the tenancy?)

Do they hand out keys to prospective tenants or do they accompany them to the property?

Can they present you with testimonial letters from current and previous clients?

What is their policy on managing arrears?

When will you receive your money?

How often do they carry out fair market rent reviews?

How will they maximise your return and optimise capital growth?

After you have found a team that meets all or most of your requirements you will be asked to appoint the agent in writing. Never proceed with an agent who does not supply or require written forms for appointment. These forms vary from state to state.

A big tip is to never go with an agent because they have the cheapest fees. In property management, service and attention to detail is far more important than saving a few extra dollars each month. Often I find agents discount their fees because they are struggling to retain business due to incompetence, or they simply do not offer a full service package. Remember, a property manager is a professional, trained and skilled to maximise your returns, to mitigate your losses, and to minimise vacancies. You want them working for you, so pay them fairly for their expertise.

Here is a great example of why you should pay for a good property manager:

> Pauline had built a new three-bedroom brick home in the northern suburbs of Brisbane and, once complete, she enquired with three local agents about their property management services. None of the three agents really differentiated themselves from each other and each one advised her that she would achieve $420 to $440 per week in rent.
>
> Pauline signed up the agent with the cheapest fees – 7.5% + GST. (Note, this was in 2010 in Queensland, and services and fees vary state to state.)
>
> The property was marketed online and Pauline had no contact from the agent for 13 days. It wasn't until she called the agent she was informed the person who signed up her business had finalised their part with her and that her property manager was called Amy.
>
> When put through to Amy, Pauline asked: "Why haven't I heard from anyone? Is my property rented yet?" Amy replied with " Pauline, no one has inspected the property and we haven't had any calls on it. At $440, the price is just too high. I think you should reduce your rent to $400, which would be more in line with the market."
>
> Pauline was confused, after all, all the agents told her it would earn between $420-$440 a week.
>
> "Why are you asking me to reduce my rent to $400?" Pauline asked.
>
> "Oh, agents will always give you a range. The top price is the most your property is worth in a really, really good market, and the lowest is what they actually think it could achieve right then and there. But in two weeks we haven't had one call and there are heaps of properties for rent in the area because of all the new houses," Amy replied.
>
> Pauline was baffled, but considering she lived in another state and wasn't fully

aware of how the rental market worked in Queensland, she agreed to reduce the rent to $400 per week.

Another four days went by and Pauline hadn't from the agent, so she called Amy and asked if anyone had applied for her house. Amy replied: "Pauline, I will call you as soon as I have an application, I promise, but right now no one is even looking at your place. Your listing is on the fourth page online and is still higher than other houses. Some four-bedroom properties are cheaper than your three-bedroom house."

Pauline was very, very disappointed. She thought she must have been sold into a 'lemon' house, nonetheless, she needed an income as mortgage payments were going out and nothing was coming in. Pauline authorised Amy to reduce the rent to $390 per week.

Three days later, Amy called Pauline and said: "I've got an application for you. It's a couple in their late 20s with three children – he works and she stays at home to watch the children." Slightly excited, Pauline asked when they were going to move in, to which Amy replied "next week".

"Well, Amy, if you have checked them out and are sure they are good tenants and can pay the rent I am happy to let them have the house. Is there anything else I should know before we start the lease?" Pauline asked. "No, Pauline, leave it to me and I will arrange everything for you," Amy said.

Amy arranged a six-month lease, signed up the tenants, and handed over the keys. The lease commenced and Amy sent a copy of the lease to Pauline. Upon receiving the lease, Pauline noticed it was only a six-month lease, even though she had stipulated a preference for 12 months in her management agreement. What's more, she noticed the tenants had two Staffordshire Bull Terrier dogs, despite requesting no pets.

Pauline called Amy to discuss the issues and, while Amy was polite and addressed all her concerns, Pauline was disappointed with the way it was handled and in herself for not asking more questions.

Unfortunately, things got worse for Pauline. Within two months of the tenancy commencing, the neighbours had called police to the property twice for noise, the Council had come and confiscated the dogs, and Amy was getting called every week by neighbours with concerns for the children and for their own wellbeing given people were coming and going at all hours. To make a bad situation worse, neighbours reported shouting inside the house. However, Pauline was never told any of this until much later.

One Thursday morning Pauline received a call from Rebekah who stated she was the agent looking after her property. Rebekah wanted to advise the tenants had moved out of the property with no notice – or at least she thought that was the case because the neighbours had just called the office.

Needless to say, Pauline was in shock. First, she wanted to know where Amy was. Rebekah advised her Amy hadn't worked in the office for six weeks and she had just taken over and was cleaning up her mess.

"What happens next?" Pauline asked, to which Rebekah replied: "I'll issue a notice to go to the house next week to make sure they have gone and then I'll take their bond for rent and cleaning. After that I'll advertise the property. You might have to get in touch with your landlord insurance company, but just wait until I tell you what we need to do."

Pauline was awfully anxious, and wasn't comforted by news from Rebekah that yes, the tenants had abandoned the property, and there was a lot of rubbish left behind. Rebekah said she would arrange the rubbish to be cleaned up and would send Pauline the invoices so she could submit her insurance claim.

Six weeks went by and Pauline had not heard from Rebekah. When she called the office she was informed Rebekah had walked out of the office two weeks ago and that Adam was looking after her property.

Pauline had had enough. She was getting very tired of her property managers chopping and changing, and she wanted answers. Upon speaking with Adam, he informed her the property was listed for rent last week and it was all sorted out. The cleaning, repairs, and rent up until the date the tenant moved out came to $4670. "But what about the rent for the last six weeks and until someone else moves in?" Pauline asked, reminding Adam the tenants left in the middle of their lease. Adam simply said: "Your insurance company will work that out for you."

That was the last straw. Pauline called a friend who she knew had property in the same area and wanted to know if their property manager was any good. He couldn't speak highly enough about her – he'd been with her for four years and she was consistent with her service. Pauline obtained that property manager's details and made the call.

When Pauline called Adam to advise she wanted to terminate management and to seek how much notice was required, Adam simply said: "Just tell the new person to come and get the keys today. I've had no enquiries on it anyway."

Given that Adam didn't want a notice period, Pauline arranged the new agent to take action immediately.

As the new agent pulled up outside the property, complete shock and disbelief hit her. The grass was knee-high, the gardens were scattered with rubbish, and the letterbox was full of mail for the old tenant. "No wonder no one has rented it, it looks derelict," she said. When she went inside, the smell hit her hard in the face. The house smelt like human waste, the walls were heavily marked, and there were patched holes as big has her head that were only roughly filled and not sanded or painted. There were long hair stands all over the floor and the tiles were sticky. The carpets were heavily stained, the wardrobe shelf in the master bedroom had collapsed, the air-conditioner no longer worked, the back sliding screen door was off the track, there was vomit on the back patio, and a saucepan-shaped burn on the kitchen bench.

The neighbour came out and approached the new agent, relaying the horrifying parties and fights, and how the old agent never did anything about it.

The agent thanked the neighbour for her information and took her number for future reference.

Pauline had advised the property was ready for tenants, but the new agent had some bad news. She took photos of the house, emailed them to Pauline and then called her. Pauline was heart broken; her five month-old property looked 15 years old, and she cried to the new agent: "What do I do?" The new agent reassured her the property would be sorted out within the week and arranged for Pauline to have the previous invoices and tenancy details. She then arranged Pauline to authorise her to deal with her insurer.

Within the week the new agent had the lawn and gardens tidied, and new photos of the outside were taken for advertising. Inside, the home was repaired and all items were attended to. In one week the home looked like a five month old home again. Just four days after the new advertising went up there were seven new enquiries on the property and an application approved and accepted for $410 per week for 12 months.

Those tenants lived in the house for 18 months before building their own property in the area. Pauline has never looked back.

That new agent was me. I didn't tell you this story to scare you from having an investment property – I can honestly say I have only been party to a handful of horror stories in the two decades I've worked in the property industry. And I didn't include the story to make me out to be Superwoman.

There are two reasons I included this story:

- ✓ If you know other investors, ask them for referrals to agents they know and trust.

- ✓ Don't base your decision on fees. While I was charging competitive rates I wasn't prepared to negotiate on fees and, realistically, the difference between me and the cheaper agents accumulated to about $8 per week. Usually agents are cheap because they need your business.

Key 2

Establishing a depreciation schedule and understanding the other tax benefits of owning an investment: What no one tells you about

One of the first things to do after buying your investment property is to arrange a depreciation schedule – even if your home isn't brand new.

Many investors have never heard of a depreciation schedule. I know I hadn't when I bought my first investment property. There are many different ways this can be explained technically as it is linked to the Australian Taxation Office (ATO), but simply put, a depreciation schedule is a list of items included in your investment property that can be depreciated at a certain rate over a period of time that you can claim as a tax deduction against your taxable income.

Another common misunderstanding is that only investors with newly built homes should obtain a depreciation schedule. This is untrue. As an investor your depreciation schedule starts from the point of settlement on your property.

Accountants are not generally qualified to prepare a depreciation schedule and, therefore, it is far better to engage a depreciation specialist. For the cost of a few hundred dollars (tax deductible dollars) you could save yourself thousands in tax dollars.

Your depreciation specialist will require an inspection of your property where he or she will note appliances, age of inclusions, brands of inclusions, take measurements of the property, and then prepare a detailed report. This report will give an accurate list and amount of what is a tax deductable depreciating item in your investment property.

What is negative gearing?

Throughout the past 12 months we've heard loads of banter in the press about negative gearing and whether the current or future governments will remove it.

Fortunately, we still have the privilege of negative gearing at this point.

Negative gearing is another term we hear of a lot when we talk about investment properties and, while it is an effective tax benefit to some investors, it is not suitable for everyone.

Basically, negative gearing means borrowing to invest – it refers to a situation where the cost of the investment property is higher than the rental return you will achieve. For example, a weekly mortgage repayment is $600 and the rental return is $450.

When you negatively gear a property you can deduct the costs of owning your investment property from your overall income and, therefore, reduce your tax bill.

Important items you can deduct include:

- Property management fees
- Interest on loans
- Landlord insurance
- Repairs and maintenance, and much more.

For more information on tax benefits for investors visit the ATO website (www.ato.gov.au).

At this stage I'm sure you already have a good understanding of whether your property is going to be negatively or positively geared. If you are unsure I cannot recommend strongly enough that you seek a qualified accountant with experience in property investment.

Key 3

Insuring your property: What options are out there?

When it comes to insuring your property, not all policies are equal.

Standard home and contents insurance will not protect against many of the risks that landlord's face. Whether it is loss of rent due to an absconding tenant, malicious or accidental damage, or a range of other circumstances including tenant hardship, risk comes in many shapes and sizes.

Insurance you need to consider:

- » **Building insurance:** This insurance must be in place before the settlement on any property. As well as fire and storm damage, you can add damage caused by tenants when a property is for investment purposes.

- » **Public liability insurance:** This is designed to protect the owner against a damages payout if anyone is injured on the premises as a result of negligence.

- » **Landlord's insurance:** Landlord's insurance is one of the most important purchases a property investor can make. For an outlay of a few hundred dollars a year, you receive cover for damage to buildings and contents, and for rental default and damage by tenants. However, as some investors have found out during the Queensland floods, it pays to make sure you get the right coverage for your property – otherwise you could be left with an expensive repair bill.

- » **Income protection:** While not compulsory, it is important to consider income protection insurance as a landlord. Could you maintain any out-of-pocket expenses on your property should you be unable to work?

There is no legal requirement from a rental/management perspective to have insurance, but take it from me, the risk is real and the insurance is imperative.

The following section provides further information about the different types of insurance relevant to investment property owners and offers a range of insurance tips.

House and contents insurance

House insurance typically covers your home, garage (and any other buildings), walls, gates, fences, and driveways. Experts recommend you have replacement cover for all included items and provision for the full cost of rebuilding.

Contents insurance covers the fittings inside your home (for example, carpets and curtains) and your personal possessions. You are not responsible for a tenant's possessions, however, it is important to cover your fixtures and fittings with your component of contents.

Landlord's insurance

You'll need landlord's insurance if you own an investment property that's being rented for residential purposes. Landlord's insurance can cover you for buildings, contents, loss of rent, rent default, theft by a tenant, and liability, among other losses. The good news is, landlord's insurance is tax deductible!

Insurance tips

1. What to look for in an insurer

The key with buying insurance is to make sure you get adequate coverage for your situation. The cost of landlord's insurance can vary wildly, with some products costing less than half that of others. However, cover and service can vary significantly. Check how and when you can claim; most insurers now operate 24-hour claim lines. Find out what you need to provide in order to claim, and what happens in worst-case scenarios (for example, if receipts are destroyed in a fire).

2. Coverage to choose

In terms of coverage, make sure you're covered for acts of nature. As has been highlighted by the recent spate of natural disasters that have affected Australia, damaging conditions can strike at any time. Therefore, it is important to ensure you're covered for the unexpected.

Events to consider coverage for:

- Storm (including damage from Lightning strike)
- Fire
- Flood (look closely at the 'type of flood' covered, for example, some policies may not cover flooding from rivers bursting their banks)
- Earthquake
- Tsunami and 'ocean movements'
- Civil unrest and rioting.

Building:

Check what your buildings cover will actually pay for. A buildings policy should protect the structure of your property, including:

- Pipes and cables
- Fixed appliances
- Gas or plumbing systems
- Fixtures and fittings (except for carpets loose floor coverings, curtains, and internal blinds)
- Exterior blinds and awnings
- Some external structures.

Building insurance should also cover you for the complete or partial destruction of the property.

Insurance becomes a little more complicated when it comes to units. As the exterior of the building is typically insured by a body corporate, you need to rely on its insurance for damage to structures. However, you can purchase specialist insurance, usually called 'strata title protection', or similar, which will cover you in the event the body corporate is underinsured.

Contents:

You should also be clear on where you stand on contents, even if you're not providing a furnished property. Contents insurance covers items that are not viewed as part of the structure of the property such as:

- Carpets
- Curtains
- Furnishings
- Furniture
- Household goods
- Internal blinds
- Loose floor coverings
- Light fittings that are not permanently fixed to the buildings
- Domestic appliances and utensils.

Rent default:

This is the most important aspect of landlord's insurance, and protects you against loss of rent. Not all policies cover all events, but most should protect you against loss of rent due to:

- Default
- Tenant eviction due to a court order
- Tenants obtaining a hardship order
- Unexpected death of tenant.

3. Insurance buyer beware

In my many years of property management, and as an investor, I have found most people take up insurance for their investment property through the company they are using for their personal home or car. While this is certainly an option, it's important to review the policy. Many insurers have what they call a 'landlord's policy', but these policies can be rife with loop holes, meaning when it comes time to make a claim, the landlord can still find themselves out of pocket.

Many of these policies only kick-in after four weeks of loss, or will charge an excess equivalent to four weeks deposit. Claim limits also vary from insurer to insurer – some will pay 12 weeks rent, others up to a full year, and others up to a fixed monetary amount.

I choose not to recommend insurers by name, but I can say I have found companies that review landlord's insurance as part of their core business typically the best providers.

4. Suggested minimum coverage

Loss of rent due to:	Cover
Denial of access	52 weeks
Prevention of access	52 weeks
Default of rent (not less than)	6 weeks
Departure without notice (not less than)	6 weeks
Breaking of lease (not less than)	6 weeks
Malicious damage	52 weeks
Accidental damage to contents	52 weeks
Accidental damage to building	2 weeks
Theft by tenant	52 weeks
Hardship (not less than)	6 weeks
Death of a tenant	52 weeks
Defined risks to contents (for example, fire and storm)	52 weeks
Damage and theft (building)	
Malicious damage	50,000
Accidental damage	$50,000
Theft by the tenant	$50,000
Damage and theft (contents)	
Malicious damage	$50,000
Accidental damage	$50,000
Theft by the tenant	$50,000
Defined risks (for example, fire and storm)	$50,000
Legal costs	**$5000**
Legal liability	30,000,000
Professional fees due to tax audit	$1000

Excess

Loss of rent	Nil
Malicious damage (not more than)	$400 per claim
Accidental damage (not more than)	$400 per event
Theft by the tenant (not more than)	$400 per claim
Legal expenses	Nil
Owner's liability	Nil
Contents fire and perils	$200 per claim (includes earthquake and cyclone)

Given the ice epidemic in Australia, I would also suggest checking if your provider offers coverage for drug lab removal and clean up as an attachment to your policy. Another option to consider is restrictions for periodic tenancies, sublet properties, or the use of short stays such as Airbnb.

Making sure you've got the right level of cover is paramount; the last thing you need is to be lying awake at night worrying about whether your policy will pay out, especially if the worst has already happened. You should never automatically assume you'll be covered and, if in doubt, it's better to be over-insured than under-insured. After all, while you may save a few hundred dollars a year with what seems to be the cheaper policy, that saving could be wiped out many times over if you end up paying-out expensive repairs that aren't covered.

The most common mistakes landlords make when insuring rental properties are:

- Buying on price – look for value not the lowest cost
- Not including deliberate fire by tenant on the policy – some policies exclude this
- Not considering excess – how much, and can the bond be used as payment?
- Underinsuring – not insuring for the true replacement value
- Not checking if malicious damage by the tenant is covered by the policy
- Not checking if accidental damage is covered by the policy – some insurers limit cover to the contents, not the building
- Not checking the qualifying rules – beware of the fine print
- Not checking for complete cover – some combined house and landlord policies offer less cover than a specialised landlord cover
- Not determining whether they need a court order to claim rent default
- Assuming the body corporate already insures the property – it might not cover liability if someone hurts themselves inside the property
- Not checking periodic tenancies or lease continuation – some policies won't pay for claims if the written lease has expired.

When you figure out "you don't need insurance" – a reliable tenant and a good property manager is not enough to protect you.*

*Information supplied by EBM Insurance Brokers

Insurance is such an important factor in protecting yourself and your investment.

Here is an example of what can and did happen.

The agent signed up a new management. The property was a lovely four-year-old brick-and-tile home in a good family area. The property manager asked the owner if they had landlord insurance and, if not, whether they would like her to arrange an insurer to contact them to discuss a policy.

The landlord simply replied: "If you are as good as you say you are there should be no need for insurance." The property manager knew she was diligent, but knowing some things are beyond her control, she said to the owner: "We do a wonderful job in vetting each and every application for you to approve; we have very strict rental arrears procedures and we religiously carry out routine inspections. However, sometimes even the best tenants can have a situation arise where they are unable to pay the rent or suffer from a mental illness brought on from a trauma such as a loss of a job or the death of a loved one – in these cases, we are unable to protect you. All we can do is keep an ear out for alarm bells and act on them quickly. I strongly recommend you consider landlord's insurance."

The owner took on board the property manager's comments and acknowledged not all situations could be controlled. Nonetheless, he proceeded without insurance. He felt he had brought into a safe area, and that landlord's insurance wasn't needed. The property manager had the owner sign a statement advising he had chosen not to take up insurance.

The property management team secured a very decent application on the property: a husband and wife in their late 30s, both professionals, with a combined income of $180,000 per annum. They had two well-mannered boys who attended a renowned private school in the area.

For the first 12 months the tenancy went like a dream. Rent was paid in advance, routine inspections went very well, and there were absolutely no alarm bells.

In the second year of the tenancy, however, the property manager arrived to do a routine inspection and, instead of the home being beautifully presented, there were wet towels on the floor, unmade beds, and dishes piled up in the sink. This wouldn't necessarily signal a bad tenant, but these guys had always made a big effort for the routine inspections.

Returning to the office, the property manager called the male tenant and asked: "Did you guys not get my notice I was coming today?" The tenant politely replied, saying he did remember, but that his wife was away for work and he was working overtime. He apologised about the state of the house, and acknowledged it wasn't as tidy as it would normally be. The property manager was okay with this explanation, didn't worry too much about the tenancy. She attached the photos on her report and noted: "House generally looked after and presented well, wife away for work so home not as well maintained as usual."

The owner never replied to the report as he was still very satisfied with the condition of the property and saw no cause for alarm.

The next routine inspection rolled around and the same property manager attended. The outside of the house looked perfect, however, when she went inside she was greeted by the male tenant who was shirtless, unshaven, and groggy as he had just woken up from the lounge. He had never been present at any previous inspections before. The house was still in reasonable condition, but it needed airing out. There were dirty clothes piling on the floor, wet towels were in the corner, dishes were piled high in the sink, and last night's dinner was still on the stove top.

Again, the tenant apologised for the state of the home, saying his wife was away with work and that he was feeling under the weather.

The property manager was getting a bit concerned. The house was really missing the 'cleaner's touch', who, in this relationship, was clearly the wife/mother. She reported the findings to the owner, but stated there were still no real concerns other than the property wasn't as tidy as it had been previously, and this must be due to the couple's workload.

Up until this point, the rent had always been paid in advance, however, the male tenant called the office to say he was going to miss next week's payment due to over-commitments. Nonetheless, he said he'd pay two weeks worth of rent the week after. As he was still in advance one week, he would still technically be up-to-date with payments, so it was acceptable to allow him to skip a week as long as he stuck to his word.

The property manager was starting to get her 'spidey senses' and called the owner to relay the situation. She advised the owner it might be wise to arrange insurance cover as she felt things were on a down-hill slide. The owner told her she was being overly cautious and that they had the bond if need be.

Two weeks later, the tenant rang the agent and said: "I've moved out of the property – I have left the keys in the letterbox. The property is empty and as is clean as I could get it."

The property manager asked him where he had moved to, and advised him of his obligations under the tenancy agreement. The tenant wouldn't tell her where he had moved to, and just said "keep my bond" before hanging up.

The agent went straight to the property to get the keys and to check the condition of the house and garden. The outside was in good condition and the inside was empty, but it required a much better clean as the windows were dirty, the bathrooms were filled with grime, and the oven was oily. There was also a fist-sized hole in the wall next to the main bedroom door.

The neighbour came out to the property manager and asked if everything was okay. The property manager simply advised the tenants had vacated.

The neighbour then proceeded to tell the property manager the wife left the husband more than six months ago. "She just walked out and left that poor man with two teenage boys," the neighbour said. "She had another fellow and she never even bothered to visit those two beautiful boys."

The property manager couldn't understand why the tenant just never told her they had parted but later worked out he lied to her as he hoped she would eventually return home.

The property manager called the owner and they immediately took action to clean up the house. Fortunately, the property was re-let in 15 days, with the total loss to the owner $2785.

Had the owner of taken insurance, it would have only cost him the cost of the annual policy, which in most cases is less than $300 and a tax deductable expense.

This could have been a much worse situation, as I have often found when tenants find themselves going through difficult times they stop communicating altogether and sometimes get aggressive (often directed at the property manager). All people react to situations differently, but denial is a major player.

There is legislation in place to protect both landlords and tenants, but issues can take time to reach resolution.

Key 4

Pricing your property and marketing your home

Most people believe what they have is far more superior to something else on the market. But when it comes to pricing your property, it's essential to be realistic.

Overpricing your property will result in lengthy vacancy periods, resulting in loss of rent. Marketing your property at market rent is the target. Regardless of what the market conditions are like, a property priced to suit its market will always find suitable tenants quickly.

There are many tools online that can help you to work out what your property is worth. However, a simple approach is to do some research online or in the real estate windows in your investment property's local area. Monitor the worth of listings in your suburb at any one time. If properties are sitting vacant for longer periods of time there could be an oversupply of stock in comparison to the demand.

Generally, there are two main reasons why a property will sit vacant and not achieve tenants:

1. **Price:** The asking price of the property is above the market. Prospective tenants cannot see value in the property at this price and, therefore, will stay in their current accommodation or take on something similar but with a more realistic price point.

2. **Marketing:** If your marketing is tardy or non-existent there will be no appeal for prospective tenants to engage your property. Remember, you can't sell a secret or, in this case, rent a secret, so engage in some marketing. Real estate websites prove to be one of the most successful strategies of getting feet through your front door.

Throughout the years I have witnessed and tried gimmicky entincement advertising where the rental market has declined and owners have wanted to maintain the previous market's income. This kind of enticement marketing includes "first week rent free", "free 32-inch TV", or "gold class movie tickets" promises. While I am a massive believer in thinking outside the square, I have found these gimmicks are unsuccessful in seducing quality tenants. A prospective tenant will rent a property that suits their needs and their budget not because they can get a $50 Myer voucher. I have never heard someone say: "I moved into my house and it's not what I needed, but I scored gold class movie tickets." In a declining market, I would recommend decreasing the rent in line with the rest of the market.

If we crunch some numbers, I am sure you will get a good understanding of price verses market.

Let's say you have a property for rent in a suburb that currently has 60 properties available, and more than a quarter of the properties are comparable. You were achieving $500 per week with the previous tenant and, therefore, have readvertised for $500 per week. However, the similar properties advertised and competing with your home are advertised at $480 per week. Prospective tenants will no doubt be attracted to the cheaper properties first, especially if they are in similar locations with similar attributes. If all the similar properties rent first and, six weeks later you approve a tenant for your home, you have just cost yourself $3000 in lost income while the home has been vacant.

If the market has declined and the price achievable for your property is now $480, my professional experience tells me you should reduce your rent to $480 per week. If a property remains advertised too long the market will think there is something wrong with it, and that no one else wants it.

By marketing the property at $480 and, let's say, it has taken two weeks to secure a new tenant (this is a fair assumption in most locations) the total loss throughout a 12-month period is $2000. Congratulations... you just saved yourself $1000!

Of course, a declining market is not a fantastic predicament and is only more common after a huge development boom or where demand has exceeded supply for long periods of time. Most commonly, we see moderate growth in investment properties yearly and, at the worst, a plateau from time to time.

With this in mind, it is important to know the different types of rental markets:

Landlord's market

This is by far the best market a landlord can ask for. This is where tenant demand exceeds supply. In this market, rents escalate, vacancies are at all-time lows and, in many instances, tenants are offering more than the asking price just to get approved.

The spin off from a landlord's market is a tenant's market. Once the market starts to change, the property will be above market rent and, at lease ends, the tenants will more than likely vacate if you do not reduce your rent back in line with the current market, leading to vacancy. In a landlord's market, it's common for tenants to over-commit themselves and arrears become an increased problem. Here, the landlord may go for several weeks with no income at all until the matter is resolved (careful tenant selection and knowing the tenant's ability to afford the rent is paramount in this style of market).

If you are realistic in your understanding that a landlord's market won't last forever, there is no shame in making hay while the sun shines, so to speak.

Balanced market

This is a comfortable market, where the supply and demand is at a constant and even level. In this market there are enough properties to cater for the amount of tenants and vice versa; rental prices are stable and will moderately increase from year-to-year. Tenants will generally have more stability and, therefore, be more likely to stay longer creating less vacancy and less wear and tear on your home. This is one of our most common markets.

Tenant market

As a landlord, this is the market we fear. This market is where you need to have a surplus of funding aside in the event your property becomes vacant. This means supply of stock far outweighs demand. Prospective tenants have the choice of multiple properties, giving the tenant the power to negotiate. Vacancies are increased and rents may be reduced.

Overall, rental markets fluctuate rapidly. Sometimes you can see a huge change week to week, whereas a sales market is generally a more gradual and longer-lasting change.

Some of the reasons rental markets rapidly change are:

- » Expiration of current leases
- » University and school holidays
- » Real estate sales prices (these days it is more acceptable for adult children to remain living at home with mum and dad for longer periods of time, especially if they are saving to purchase a home. However, if they are simply living there for an easy life it seems less common the adult child will vacate the family home due to the pressure to leave his/her parents. Having said that, if rental prices are steady, the adult child might choose to move out for their own freedom)
- » Employment cycles
- » Reduced interest rates.

Key 5

Presentation:
You don't get a second chance to make a first impression

After you have researched the market and decided on an achievable rental price, it's time to ensure the property you are about to rent is ready for occupancy.

Even before the advertising and marketing has commenced, ensure your home's presentation is appealing. At the end of the day, you want prospective tenants to want your home and getting them through the front door is the first step.

Some things to consider:

- Keep the lawns mowed, edged and free-from any green waste. Weed all gardens and mulch to create a fresh, easy maintenance appeal. Ensure the driveway is gurnied and free of dirt and grease, and make sure the outside of the home is clean by knocking down any cobwebs and cleaning the windows.
- If there are trees or shrubs around the home, prune and shape them. If they have been rubbing or growing close to gutters, make sure the gutters are cleared and rust-free.
- Ensure fences and gates are secure, safe and sturdy – not only will this appeal to tenants with children or pets, it will also eliminate safety issues.
- Make sure there is a number present on the house or letter box, as prospective tenants need to be able to find your home quickly and easily.

Once you have appealed to prospective tenants from the outside you need to ensure the inside follows through with the good presentation. Poor presentation will result in longer vacancies, lower rent, and a lower calibre of tenant. If a tenant moves in to a home that is tired, needs maintenance, or looks tardy, it can also become easy for them to relax with the presentation while they live there. Lead by example!

**Ensure the property is clean – not just dusted, but commercially clean.
Make sure you:**

- Wash down walls or give a fresh coat of paint to remove grubby marks: If you decide to paint, choose a neutral colour (cream, beige or white). Bright colours might be the flavour of the era, but they will date and your taste may not be to the market's liking.

- Have the carpets professionally steam cleaned.

- Make sure the kitchen is spotless: Clean all surfaces inside and outside of cupboards, remove all oil and baked-on grime from the oven, degrease the range-hood, run a rinse aid through the dishwasher, and shine the sink and any other stainless steel appliances to make them sparkle.

- Scrub toilets and bathrooms: Getting rid of soap scum and residue from your shower screens is a must. If any taps, pipes, or shower heads are leaking, get them fixed straight away.

- Remember to clean light shades, skirting boards, windows, window sills, and window tracks.

- The patio forms part of the home, as do any sheds, garages, or external areas – so clean these too.

- Fix anything that is broken such as cracked tiles, blown lights, or loose door handles. Not only will this make the property appealing for prospective tenants, but you have peace of mind that when a tenant takes occupancy they will comfortably move in without the hassle of reporting maintenance work straight away.

I understand everyone has a different understanding of clean and, while you might be happy to move into the home, would your tenant? Sometimes it is best to engage a cleaning company to do a full clean of the premises prior to marketing and leasing. Your agent should be able to recommend a cleaner that understands the quality required. If you are a do-it-yourself (DIY) landlord, ensure you engage a reputable company that guarantees their work.

Unless you are letting out your home as a furnished package, ensure the property – including any sheds – is empty. Do not leave any belongings of any description, including pot plants or garden ornaments. Anything left at the property becomes an inclusion and if it breaks or wears out, you will have to replace or repair it.

By having high standards in presentation, you are more likely to achieve a tenant far more quickly than the competing properties, possibly obtain a longer-term tenant, receive a premium rent, and get a better calibre of tenant. In my many years of property management I have conducted inspections for vacant properties where prospective tenants who have looked at several homes have made positive comments on the condition and presentation of the home I am marketing. During my career I have even refused to market properties that have not met my high standards.

As I am such a stickler for processes, I feel it is only fitting that I give you a checklist to use when preparing your property for rent. Copy the next page as many times as you need and, if you think of anything else, I would love your feedback.

Items to take care of if you lived in the property prior to renting it out:

- » Have your mail re-directed
- » Disconnect or cancel your utilities
- » Leave a copy of your appliance manuals on the kitchen bench
- » Ensure all locks have keys and there are at least two full sets of keys.

Cleaning guide

- Walls: Clean off dirty marks, scuffs etc. Repaint full walls if they are damaged.
- Mould: Ensure all mould is removed from ceilings, walls, and the bathroom.
- Light fittings: Wash all lights shades, remove cobwebs and bugs, and ensure light globes work.
- Skirtings, doors and window frames: Clean off dust or marks.
- Windows: Wash windows inside and out.
- Window screens: Ensure mesh is not torn and wipe away dust.
- Kitchen: Remove all grease from splashbacks, clean oven, range hood and stove, polish sink, make sure plugs are present, and wipe out all cupboards and surfaces.
- Bathrooms: Remove all soap scum, shine tap ware, clean toilets, and replace seats.
- Laundry: Clean under tubs, and polish tap ware and sinks.
- Bedrooms and lounge: Clear out all cupboards, and vacuum carpets.
- Fans and air-conditioning: Clean out air conditioning filters, wipe over fan blades (top and bottom).
- Curtains and blinds: Launder all curtains, replace anything torn, clean down blinds, and make sure tracks work and chains are intact.
- Floors: Mop all tiles and vinyl, vacuum all carpets, and ensure carpets are professionally cleaned (it's a good idea to provide the receipt to your managing agent).
- Lawns: Mow and edge all lawns.
- Gardens: Remove all weeds, trim all shrubs, and mulch.
- Guttering: Clean out the gutters, and repair broken down pipes.
- Paths and driveways: Remove weeds from between pavers, degrease and gurney driveways.
- Garage and sheds: Remove all objects, knock down cobwebs, and sweep out the areas.
- Pests: Have the property sprayed for cockroaches, spiders, and silverfish, and provide the receipt to agent.
- Overall, make sure all areas are safe and in good condition.

Key 6

Securing a tenant: Get the best pick of the bunch

Securing a tenant is the most important aspect when it comes to your property producing an income. However, gone are the days where a tenant hands over a key deposit and goes and inspects the property. A lease is no longer a handshake deal.

Tenants must be vetted to ensure they are of a high calibre and are capable of paying the rent and maintaining your home. The various Acts governing residential tenancies outline landlord obligations and tenant responsibilities.

It is important prospective tenants view the property to ensure it meets their requirements; if the tenant is unable to view the property then have them arrange someone they trust to do so on their behalf. Alternatively, have the tenant sign a waiver that stipulates they accept the property sight unseen.

It is absolutely imperative the tenant fills in an application form and provides identification.

The application should have provisions such as:

- Applicant details such as names, dates of birth, address, phone and email contact, licence number, passport number, dependants, and the type and number of vehicles that will be parked at the property

- Current accommodation details: If the prospective tenant is currently renting, request the details of their current agent or private landlord (if renting through a private landlord, run a search to see the accommodation is actually owned by the person the prospective tenant has identified as the landlord). If the prospective tenant is living in their own property and it has been sold or is being sold, request the details of the sales agents and run a search to verify that the prospective tenants do in fact own said property

- Past accommodation details (as above)

- Employment details (how long they have been employed, weekly/annual income, and position stability. If self-employed, seek a financial statement or verification from their accountant)

- Personal reference details and a next-of-kin contact.

Have the prospective tenants sign a disclosure statement allowing you to obtain information about them from the sources listed on the application, such as real estate agents, employers, and references. A disclosure statement also allows you to check the tenants through specialised tenancy and credit databases such as TICA and the National Tenancy Database (NTD).

Important

Where possible, obtain a copy of a rental ledger. This is evidence the tenant has a history of paying rent on time.

Thoroughly checking applications is imperative. Keeping a record of the findings is just as important as you can use this information later should the need arise to pursue insurers or debt collectors.

Long-term lease v short-term tenancy

There are no rules stating a lease must be six or 12 months. A lease can be three months, 14 months or five years. In fact, as long as both parties agree, a lease can be whatever length is suitable.

A short-term lease could be useful where a prospective tenant is building their own home or is intending on leaving the area shortly. Generally, short-term tenancies will mean further marketing costs, slightly more wear and tear with the tenant moving in and out, and another vacancy within a short timeframe. While you may be able to seek a higher return for a short-term rental agreement, you need to weigh up the pros and cons. Consider if the property is in a holiday area, or a short-stay area.

A long-term lease offers income security for a fixed period, assisting you with planning and budgeting. A long-term lease generally means less wear and tear on the property, and less expenditure on advertising and costs associated with re-letting. Personally, I strive for longer-term leases (generally 24 months not ending in December) as these suit my personal budgeting and the properties I have are not located in short-stay areas.

Depending on the location of your property, it may be more beneficial to furnish your home and offer it as a 'whole deal'. Furnished homes are mainly suitable for holiday lettings, however, if the home is in a location that attracts fly-in/fly-out miners or business executives, a long-term tenancy for a furnished home might be desirable.

There is no right or wrong answer when it comes to determining the length of your lease. What you need to do is study your area, speak to agents in the know, and make a decision based on your own unique circumstances.

Paperwork: It must be done

Once you and your tenant have agreed on a tenancy, there are three non-negotiable items a landlord or property manager must do:

1. Take an appropriate bond and lodge it with the authority for that state.

2. Sign a tenancy agreement outlining the expectations of the tenancy and how and when rent is to be paid.

3. Write an in-going report, taking note of the current condition of the property. This will give you evidence at the end of the tenancy of how the property should be returned.

Hot tip

Attach photos to your in-going report and date them.

Each state's authority will be able to provide the appropriate paperwork for the start of a tenancy, and most items will be free to obtain. Your agent will have all of the necessary documents as well as other best practice forms to ensure there are no miscommunications or unknown expectations during the tenancy.

Paperwork requires a high level of attention to detail and know-how. Again, I stress the need to engage a qualified professional manager.

Key 7

Maintaining that tenant: A little respect goes a long way

One of the most common complaints made by tenants is that they feel like second class citizens. Some tenants feel landlords and property agents don't respect them, and that many also fail to establish a good rapport with them.

While it is important to keep a business mindset, it is essential to remember you are dealing with people; people who have housing needs and who assist us as landlords in fulfilling our investment dream. Trust me; in my life I have been a tenant, a landlord, and an agent, and so I have seen all perspectives!

In the previous chapter I touched on making sure there are no unknown expectations for the tenancy; if this is done from the start, the rest of the tenancy will be a lot more hassle-free.

Remember, without tenants landlords would have no income from their properties, so we need to be able to show consideration and good sense on matters relating to tenants. While you may own the property, it is your tenant's home for the life of the lease, so allow them to make it theirs (within reason, of course).

Here are a few suggestions to help create a good relationship with your tenant/s:

- » Advise the tenants upon moving in they are allowed to put up, for example, four picture hooks per room. For anything else, they should seek your permission in writing or use removable hooks.

- » Allow tenants the privilege of installing pay TV as long as it is professionally done and at their expense. In today's world, pay TV is almost a standard utility.

- » When wanting to inspect the property, make sure you do it within the guidelines of your state's legislation. Over-inspecting becomes intimidating and can verge on harassment. If you are allowed, by law, to do four inspections per year then utilise them but be courteous and ensure the proper notification is issued in writing, as well as by phone.

- » At the inspection, ask the tenant if there is anything they think requires refurbishment or installing to help them feel at home. While you do not have to commit to the tenant's suggestions, the tenant will feel important and valued.

- » Prior to the end of the tenancy, contact the tenant and find out what they are planning to do and how they are situated moving forward. Research the market and put forward a proposal to the tenant to renew. If the current rent is below market rent and you do not want a vacancy, approach them with a new lease with a moderate increase. This could be viewed as a win-win. Alternatively, notify the tenant that the rent needs to be increased to market rent but offer them one or two weeks rent for free – again, a win-win situation. Remember nothing is black or white in property management and it is all about negotiating until both parties agree.

When it comes to maintaining your tenant, communication is key. Direct, friendly, and informative contact will help create an atmosphere of mutual respect, and the tenancy will most likely be hassle-free.

Engaging a property manager will remove you from this situation so when you are trying to negotiate you are not face-to-face with the tenant and, therefore, less likely to make emotionally-based decisions.

Key 8

Property maintenance: During the tenancy, sometimes you have to spend a little to make a lot

Maintenance is an essential part of owning an investment property, however it's not only good for monetary growth.

Maintenance during a tenancy should be handled professionally for a number of reasons, including:

- » Prevention of public liability and indemnity claims
- » Legal obligations as a lessor
- » Respect for your tenant and the property.

In each state, there will be different guidelines on what is classified as a emergency repair and what is a standard repair. These guidelines will also stipulate timeframes for lessors to action repairs, along with the obligations of the tenant, and processes in the event the lessor refuses action or the tenant hinders repairs or maintenance.

Have a budget in place that incorporates unforseen expenses per month so you are not caught in a position where you cannot action a repair that you are obliged to attend.

It's important to note, DIY repairs could be just as costly, if not more so in the long-term, than engaging a professional tradesperson.

You or your appointed agent should have a maintenance policy in place and this should be addressed with the tenant when they first move in.

This policy could be along the lines of:

- » The tenant should submit maintenance requests in writing (dated and signed, with photos, where possible).
- » In the event of an emergency on the weekend or in the middle of the night, the tenant should consult a list of professionals pre-approved by the landlord/property manager. If for any reason those tradespeople do not respond, the tenant can contact someone they choose. Stipulate this can only be done for emergency repairs and that if the tenant calls out a tradesperson on their own accord for general repairs they will be billed or held responsible for the afterhours call-out fee.

As the landlord, you are obligated to conduct maintenance to the property. It is particularly important to immediately investigate any item that is reported that could be deemed dangerous or harmful to any persons at the property. Always document these actions.

Remember not to get complacent with your maintenance. Even if you think you are taking reasonable and timely action, your tenant may have other ideas. If they put forward a claim for compensation or liability, you will have to have evidence to show what measures you took to resolve the matter – so document your actions.

Minor maintenance, such as loose door handles or leaky taps, can be frustrating. However, these are just as important to get fixed quickly. If the tenant sees you are a conscientious landlord they will more than likely uphold their obligations in reporting maintenance and, at times, may even take initiative in minor repairs themselves.

Don't ever wish or encourage your tenant not to report maintenance!

Here is a story of how it went wrong for an old friend of mine.

Col owned a property in a small rural town. The property was old and dated, however, it was maintained in a tidy condition and its rent reflected its age.

Col had the property rented through a local agent but insisted on doing his own maintenance and often got to know his tenants.

When the tenants would report leaking taps or other maintenance issues it would generally take him a few weeks before he could attend. Due to this relaxed attitude with maintenance the tenants became less active in terms of reporting, and would put up with maintenance issues for lengthy periods before notifying the owner or the agent.

At one point, the kitchen tap spout started to leak at the base plate attached to the wall whenever the tenant turned on the cold tap. The tenants weren't bothered by this, therefore, didn't think it was worth reporting. After all, they knew how busy Col was and that it would take him weeks to come and 'dodgy up' the leak.

As the months went by, mould began to grow in the grout from the area being damp all the time. The tenant put Exit Mould on the tiles as part of their weekly clean and thought nothing more of it. Then, suddenly, the tiles on the sink splashback started to fall off the wall around the taps. At this point the tenants decided it was time to advise the agent and Col.

Three weeks after the work was reported and seven months after the initial leak occurred, Col went to fix the problem. He thought it would be as simple as sticking the tiles back in place. However, upon his visit to the property he found the Gyprock behind the tiles had become so damp and mouldy he could push his finger through it. He decided he needed a professional tiler to replace the Gyprock, and re-tile the area.

When the tiler came and removed the Gyprock, the sub-frame to the wall was rotten and infested with termites. Now, a termite treatment was required and a builder needed to be contracted to restructure the sub-frame.

The kitchen was unusable while the work was conducted.

The total cost of these repairs

Plumber to stop the leak	$66
Termite inspector	$490
Builder	$1,130
Tiler	$330
Tenant compensation	$140
Total:	**$2,165**

If the leaking spout had been fixed when it was first noticed, the total cost of repair would have been $66 for the plumber.

Key 9

Property maintenance: Between tenancies, you can make mutton look like lamb

It is vitally important to ensure your home is maintained between tenancies. Have regard for the condition of the property as stated in '*Key 5: Property presentation*' because, once again, appeal is essential to attracting great tenants.

Generally, you will want a quick turnaround of tenants and, if you live interstate or have a busy lifestyle, it may be difficult to inspect the property and to attend to items that need touching-up.

In my time as a property manager, I have had several landlords attend vacate inspections or visit the property while it is untenanted, and I find many of these landlords have unrealistic expectations. As a landlord, you must remember the property must be left in the same condition as it was let, allowing for fair wear and tear. This is where some landlords get emotional; they visit the property for the first time after a tenant has lived there for two years and are disappointed in the condition of the property and, in many instances, blame the agent for allowing the tenant to leave without fulfilling their obligations. I would suggest that in 90% of these cases the agent hasn't failed in their duties, rather the owner is not considering wear and tear on a home that has been lived in for a period of time. Yes, there will be blemishes on walls, some grout discolouration, track marks in the carpets, and possibly disintegration of dials on stoves – but this is part and parcel of owing an investment property.

> I can assure you there is a clear and noticeable difference between tenant neglect and wear and tear.

As the home gets older and has more tenants coming in and out of it, the home will age – generally this will be at a faster rate than that of your own home. This is why in-going and out-going reports are paramount, and photos are an excellent way to compare and keep maintenance matters clear.

So with all that said and done, it is important as a landlord to maintain the property between tenancies. Ask your agent to give you a list of items that have been noted during routine inspections that you didn't attend to for whatever reason, and to provide recommendations to ensure the property is in excellent condition to attract new tenants.

Again these suggestions could be anything from:

- » Clearing gutters
- » Pruning trees
- » Putting new numbers on the letter box
- » Washing the exterior of the house and driveway
- » Replacing corroded taps
- » A quick coat of paint (for older homes)
- » Replacing faded curtains or blinds.

These examples would mainly occur in homes that have been tenanted longer than 12 months and are ageing. If you've only had tenants for a six-month tenancy and you have attended to maintenance issues during that period, it's likely you won't have anything to attend to.

In the event of high vacancy periods, ensure you arrange a lawn mowing person to attend, at least fortnightly, to keep the grass low and the garden tidy. This way, it won't be as obvious that the property is vacant and it will be more appealing to tenants. The neighbours will be happy as well!

Here is a basic budget to help you crunch some numbers:

Maintenance or refurbishment item	Estimated cost	Expected due date	Annual saving	Weekly savings	Date completed
Replace carpets through out	$3,000.00	5 years 2020	$600.00	$11.53	
Replace carpet					
Replace hot water system					
Replace window coverings					
Internal painting					
External painting					
Replace gutters					
Refurbish gardens					
Replace fly screens					
Replace dishwasher					
Service air-conditioner					
Service remote garage doors					
Service pool					
Replace pool equipment					
Replace light fittings					
Re-seat tap ware					
Roof restoration					
Kitchen cupboard hinge and handle replacements					
Fence replacement/repair					
Yearly miscellaneous repairs budget					

Totals

Key 10

How can you make money from your property?

1. Negative gearing v positive gearing… we need to watch this space!

There are many different ideas about how you can make money out of property. However, there are really only two real ways to make a profit:

1. Rental income.
2. Capital growth.

Rental income puts money directly into your account, but only if the rent exceeds the costs associated with having the property. Properties that earn more than they cost are called 'positive cash flow' properties. Generally, they have a yield of 9% or higher.

(NB: To calculate your yield divide your annual rent by the purchase price multiplied by 100 =? %

Example $30,160 ÷ $580,000 = 0.052 x 100 = 5.2%)

Capital growth is where the property increases in value throughout the period of years held. Therefore, if you were to sell the property or have the property valued, you would make a profit.

There are pros and cons for both, so let's have a look at what they are and then examine other ways to sustain growth and weather any storms.

Positive cash flow

Generally, it tends to be difficult to find or have a property that is positively geared upfront. However, if you are in this position you will find income from this property will be taxed, which may not allow you to create wealth quickly.

Positive cash flow properties are also generally found in rural or remote areas where capital growth is often much longer and the rental market more volatile.

However, there is much to be said about paying tax – it means you are earning money!

Capital growth

Holding on to a property long-term will generally result in profit if the property is held long enough. Usually properties situated in the city or in high population areas will have a higher, more consistent growth, and this would result in the investor generating equity more quickly. The disadvantage of these properties is that during the holding period they will cost money. The government to offer tax benefits for having a negatively geared property.

So is one better than the other? While most experts recommend following a growth strategy so that you can increase your portfolio, it depends on what suits your needs. At the end of the day, we just want to be making money, or creating wealth for the future.

2. Minor and major improvements to boost your rental return: Getting more bang for your buck

Not every day is a good day in the investment world. Sometimes the market can plateau, or worse, rental prices can decrease. Whatever the condition is, you need to ensure you will receive an income from your rental property, that you can weather the storm, and that you can get back into the growth season.

Keeping long-term tenants in a high vacancy period, or simply achieving more rent are good ways to weather a plateau in the market.

Here are some ideas:

- A good outside spruce-up – paint eaves and roofs, clean gutters, paint fences, and tidy and mulch the gardens
- Revamp tap ware and door handles
- Replace kitchen appliances, if tardy – a new stovetop can get you over the line
- One coat of paint can quickly cover scuffs and brighten up the property
- Put in new carpet – it's fresh and appealing.

None of these ideas would cost more than $1000, and it's often the smallest touches that make a property that much more appealing.

Other adjustments to improve the return on your investment could include:

- Allowing the investor to increase the rent at lease renewal time for the same tenant
- Allowing the investor to achieve a higher return than other properties in the area that are lacking appeal
- Enticing long-term tenants where rent can be moderately increased yearly
- If the property becomes vacant the investor will generally have a shorter vacancy period.

Major works to boost growth include:

- If in a desired location, furnish the property but with a few real quality pieces
- Go solar – install at least a 5kW solar system on the property
- Install air-conditioning – a big enough unit to do the full home or a ducted system
- If your property is small, basic and could do with renovations, consider:
  - ✓ Create a second bathroom or ensuite
  - ✓ Put in a separate laundry
  - ✓ Add on an entertainment area
  - ✓ Put up a carport or a garage
  - ✓ Add storage.

While these improvements have a much higher cost to the investor, they are likely to add value for the tenants. When it comes time to sell the property, you will also receive a much better sale price or valuation.

Before spending any money, it is important to seek professional advice about the benefit you will receive in terms of both capital growth and rental return.

Sustaining your rental return isn't just about spending money, it's also about keeping your tenants in place and minimising vacancy periods.

It is important you are realistic about rental values and understand the market and where your property sits in the marketplace. Some landlords can have an unrealistic view of what their properties are worth, and these unrealistic expectations can cost you money or sour your investment experience.

Another way to ensure you can weather any storm is to refinance your property to create a cash buffer. Obviously, this can only be done when your property grows in value. At no point do you want to be forced into a sale due to the loss of your job or other circumstances, as you won't get the best price and you could be hit with capital gains tax, which would remove any profits from the sale.

Creating a cash buffer will ensure you have the funds to continue to maintain your property and pay your mortgage during your hardship.

There are highly skilled professional financial planners and advisors available who can help you work out the best way to move forward at any one time.

You don't have to go through this investment adventure on your own.

Everyone wants your investment property to be a success – it's good for you, it's good for the agent, it's good for the tenant and, in my opinion, it's good for the economy.

Key 11

The round up

We are coming to the end of the book and I hope the information provided has been helpful and assists you in making the most out of your investment property.

Growing a property portfolio is exciting and, generally, you will find you get the 'investing bug', as I like to call it. Once I had my first property, I couldn't wait to get my second and so on. The more involved I got, the more I loved it and was able to make really informed decisions.

I seemed to have an influence on friends and they caught the bug too.

My investment properties have enabled me to get to where I am today and, in some instances, have allowed me to maintain financial security while others who didn't have investments were left starting from scratch.

This is not good bye, it's see you later. I'd love to hear from you and learn all about your investment success stories.

Samara Bedwell

Let me leave you with a list of
investor mantras

I won't treat my property like a hobby.

I will create rapport with the tenant but without emotion.

I wont treat the property like it is the home we live in but understand it is a business.

I will maintain the property.

I will get a depreciation schedule.

I will increase the rents regularly but not excessively.

I will pay down non-deductable debts before deductable debts.

I will work with a good accountant.

I will get adequate insurance cover.

I will get professionals to handle the management side of my property.

I won't lose sight of the big picture.

I can do this!

Quick links and resources

If you're looking for an ethical agent who complies with best practice, look for an agent who is a member of your state's Real Estate Institute.

REIACT
16 Thesiger Court
Deakin ACT 2600
- 02 6282 4544
- 02 6285 1960
- reiact@reiact.com.au
- www.reiact.com.au

REIWA
215 Hay Street
Subiaco WA 6008
- 08 9380 8222
- 08 9381 9260
- admin@reiwa.com.au
- www.reiwa.com.au
  www.commerce.wa.gov.au/consumer-protection/property-industry

REISA
249 Greenhill Road
Dulwich SA 5065
- 08 8366 4300
- 08 8366 4380
- reisa@reisa.com.au
- www.reisa.com.au/
  www.cbs.sa.gov.au

REIT
33 Melville Street
Hobart TAS 7000
- 03 6223 4769
- 03 6223 7748
- admin@reit.com.au
- www.reit.com.au/
  www.consumer.tas.gov.au/property/real_estate_agent

REINT
Unit 3/6 Lindsay Street
Darwin NT 0801
- 08 8981 8905
- 08 8981 3683
- info@reint.com.au
- www.reint.com.au/

REIV
335 Camberwell Road
Camberwell VIC 3124
- 03 9205 6666
- 03 9205 6699
- reiv@reiv.com.au
- www.reiv.com.au/
  www.consumer.vic.gov.au/estateagentscouncil

REIQ
21 Turbo Drive
Corporoo QLD 4151
- 07 3249 7347
- 07 3249 6211
- reception@reiq.com.au
- www.reiq.com
  www.qld.gov.au/law/fair-trading/

REINSW
30-32 Wentworth Avenue
Sydney South NSW 2000
- ?
- 02 9267 9190
- ?
- www.reinsw.com.au
  www.fairtrading.nsw.gov.au

Other important links
www.yourinvestmentpropertymag.com.au
www.eurekareport.com.au

www.rentcover.com.au
www.afr.com
www. ppmgroup.com.au/

PROPERTY MANAGEMENT

PO Box 1167, Capalaba QLD 4157
07 3180 3209
service@macwell.com.au

www.macwell.com.au

ISBN 978-0-6484117-1-0

www.ingramcontent.com/pod-product-compliance
Ingram Content Group UK Ltd.
Pitfield, Milton Keynes, MK11 3LW, UK
UKHW021255180426
11947UKWH00011B/800